THESE JOBS ARE **NOT INCREDIBLE.** THEY ARE JUST **SILLY!**

For Jessica, who has done an incredible job with us all! – M.B.

For my agent Maria, who has been there every step of my way. – F.H.

A TEMPLAR BOOK

First published in the UK in 2025 by Templar Books,
an imprint of Bonnier Books UK
5th Floor, HYLO, 103-105 Bunhill Row,
London, EC1Y 8LZ
Owned by Bonnier Books
Sveavägen 56, Stockholm, Sweden
www.bonnierbooks.co.uk

Text copyright © 2025 by Mike Barfield
Illustration copyright © 2025 by Franziska Höllbacher
Design copyright © 2025 by Templar Books

10 9 8 7 6 5 4 3 2 1

All rights reserved

ISBN 978-1-80078-373-7

This book was typeset in Providence Sans,
Bokka, Chubby Chap and Mind Boggle.
The illustrations were created digitally.
Edited by Sophie Hallam
Fact-checked by Elaine Rhodes
Designed by Anna Ring
Production by Neil Randles

Printed in China

THE WORLD'S FIRST HUMAN CANNONBALL

AND OTHER INCREDIBLE JOBS

MIKE BARFIELD

templar books

FRANZISKA HÖLLBACHER

CONTENTS

1 GOING PLACES 9
INCAN MESSENGER 10
CHARIOT RACER 12
RED FLAG LAD 14
BESSIE COLEMAN 16
SPACEMAN 18
BROUGHT TO BOOK 20

FEATURING BESSIE COLEMAN ON PAGE # 16 #

2 BODY WORK 21
MUMMY MAKER 22
BARBER-SURGEON 24
TOAD EATER 26
MARIE TUSSAUD 28
HUMANOID 30
STAND-OUT STAND-INS 32

FEATURING MARIE TUSSAUD ON PAGE 28

3 NICE WORK 33
COURT JESTER 34
PLUTOCRAT 36
HERMIT 38
GRUMPY CAT 40
EASY MONEY 42

FEATURING GRUMPY CAT ON PAGE # 40 #

4 RISKY BUSINESS 43
NORSE FAMER 44
PIRATE 46
ZAZEL 48
ESCAPOLOGIST 50
MINE-FINDING RAT 52
DANGER MONEY 54

FEATURING ZAZEL ON PAGE # 48 #

5 WORKING WONDERS
- ORACLE 55
- JAMES RANDI 56
- PROGNOSTICATOR 58
- WORKS LIKE A CHARM 60
.... 62

FEATURING JAMES RANDI ON PAGE # 58 #

6 WORK HARD, PLAY HARD
- MARTIAL ARTIST 63
- AZTEC BALL GAME PLAYER 64
- LILY PARR 66
- COSTUME DRAMA 68
.... 70

FEATURING LILY PARR ON PAGE # 68 #

7 ARTS WORK
- ACTOR 71
- MODERN ARTIST 72
- FILM STAR 74
- WILLIAM MCGONAGALL 76
- HANDIWORK 78
.... 80

FEATURING WILLIAM MCGONAGALL ON PAGE 78

8 DIRTY WORK
- FULLER 81
- GONG FARMER 82
- JOSEPH PUJOL 84
.... 86

FEATURING JOSEPH PUJOL ON PAGE # 86 #

- 88
- YOU HAD ONE JOB 90
- EARLY STARTERS 92
- CAREER PATH

INTRODUCTION

Hello, and CONGRATULATIONS on winning the very important job of

READER-IN-CHIEF

of this book!

READER-IN-CHIEF

YOUR PHOTO GOES HERE

NAME: ???????
NATIONALITY: ??????
OCCUPATION: READER-IN-CHIEF

It's an exciting position that comes with lots of great rewards!

The hours are flexible. You can dip in and out at any time that suits you, day or night. All we ask in return is that you learn a little and laugh a lot as we reveal the astonishing stories behind...

The First Human Cannonball and Other Incredible Jobs.

From ancient Egypt to modern times, the whole wide world of work lies between these pages — from the strange to the dangerous and even out into space!

So, grab a chair and get to work. It'll certainly pay you back in facts and laughs. Plus, this book won't read itself, you know!

CHAPTER 1
GOING PLACES

Early humans moved around in search of food. Simply surviving was a job in itself. Since we settled down, there have been lots of odd occupations, past and present, that involve transport or travel. That's what this first chapter is all about, so here are four fab facts to get you going!

LEAST EASY CHAIR

Sedan chairs carried fashionable people across filthy city streets over 200 years ago. The chairs were heavy, rides were bumpy and accidents often occurred!

WORLD'S LONGEST SHIP

Scrapped in 2009, the Seawise Giant oil tanker was four football pitches long. Its captain always planned ahead, as the ship took 9 km to come to a halt.

HEAVIEST LAND VEHICLE

US space agency NASA uses huge crawler-transporters to take rockets to their launch sites. Due to the extremely heavy weight, it has a top speed of 1.6 km/hour. No speed fiends need apply!

FIRST AIR STEWARDS

For men, starting in 1912, German Heinrich Kubis served on giant Zeppelin airships. For women, American Ellen Church (a trained pilot) began stewarding planes in 1930.

INCAN MESSENGER

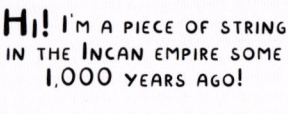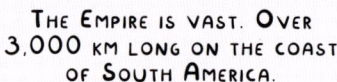

JUST THE JOB: GET THE MESSAGE

WINGING IT
Winston the pigeon became a celebrity in South Africa in 2009 when he flew home 96 km with a 4 GB memory stick faster than the data could be downloaded online. Coo!

HIGH OFFICE
The China Postal Service runs the world's highest post office at Base Camp on Mount Everest. Climbers can send postcards in warmer months. Wish you were there?

DRONING ON!
Drones are already replacing delivery drivers in hard-to-reach places around the world. In Rwanda, Africa, they carry medical supplies — just what the doctor ordered!

DON'T MISS THE BOAT!
A mailboat on Lake Geneva, Wisconsin, USA, keeps moving slowly along the shoreline, while young 'mail-jumpers' jump off and on stuffing mailboxes on piers. Sometimes they fall in!

CHARIOT RACER

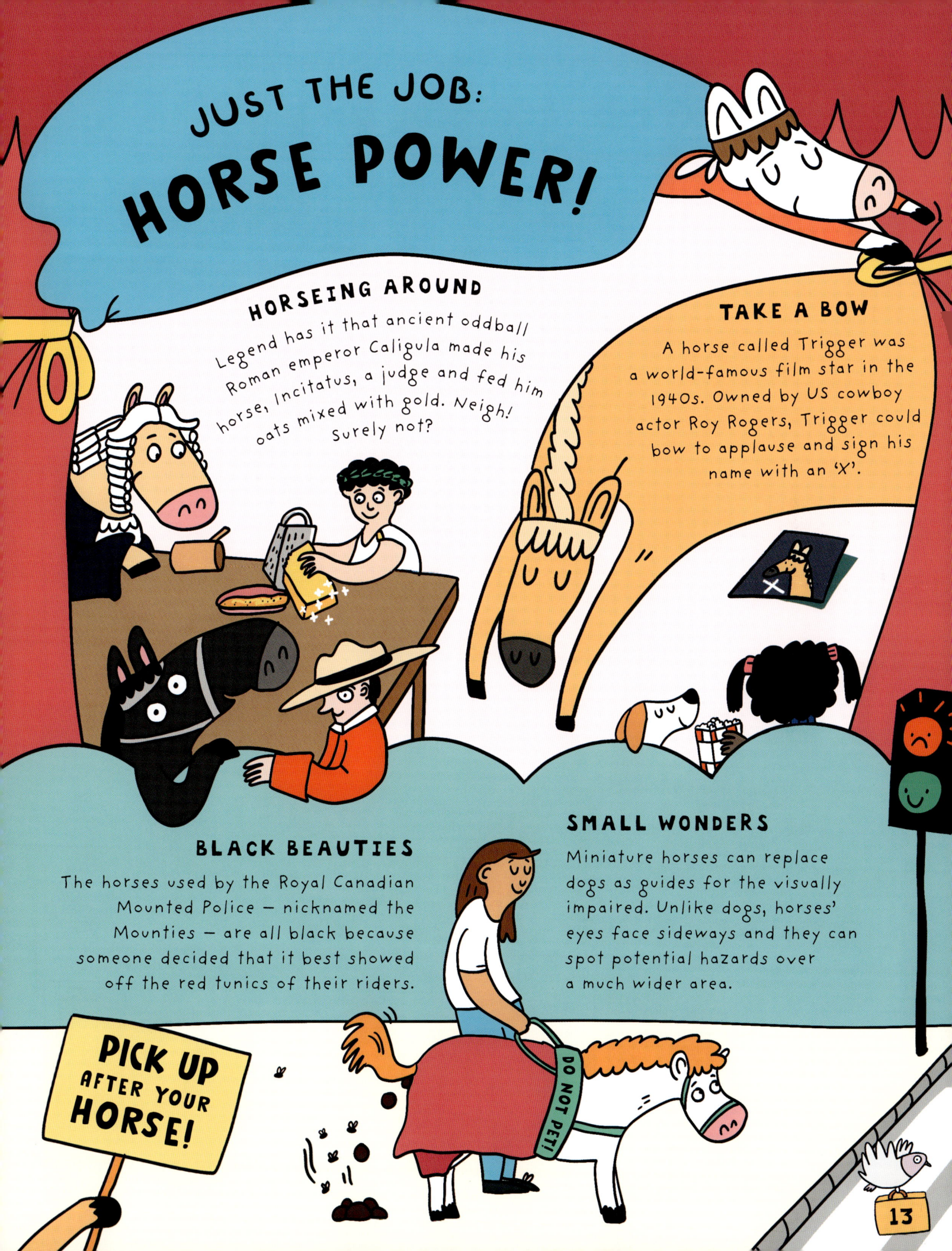

RED FLAG LAD

Hi! I'll come to the point. I'm a pencil, and this story is true.

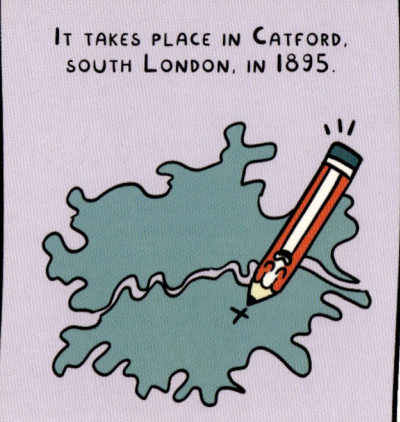

It takes place in Catford, south London, in 1895.

This innocent-looking boy is working as a look-out...

CHUG! CHUG!

I'm a fine-looking look-out, if I say so myself, guv!

He is looking out for police officers, who are looking out for motor cars like the one behind him...

HELLO, HELLO, HELLO!

It belongs to Henry Hewetson who hates going slowly.

I feel a need for speed!

But the law says he can't go faster than 2 MPH* in town.

* 3.2 KM/HOUR

Plus, you're meant to have someone in front waving a red flag to warn people...

WHAT HAVE WE HERE?

So, when the look-out spots the officer, he signals to the car, which slows to let the passenger out, who is carrying... me!

The law does not say what size the flag needs to be!

HA! BAH!

The speed limit was raised soon after — and I bet cars go much faster in the future... Don't they?

FAST FORWARD TO YOUR TIME!

GRRR! TRAFFIC JAM!

HONK! HONK!

STUCK!

JUST THE JOB: DRIVE TIME

CHILL OUT!
Truckers supplying mines in northern Canada have to drive over frozen lakes and rivers. The trick is to never stop moving or you might break the ice. Eek!

HOP IT!
Truckers in the intense heat of the Australian outback hitch together several trailers to create huge 'road trains' that can't stop in a hurry. Kangaroos, keep out of their way!

CLOWNING AROUND
German-born Lou Jacobs invented the one-person clown car in the 1950s. He could squeeze inside and drive it around despite being 1.85 m tall and the car just 90 cm long.

QUACKERS!
Many cities have so-called 'duck tours' where special amphibious buses take sightseers through rivers, lakes and harbours, as well as on regular roads!

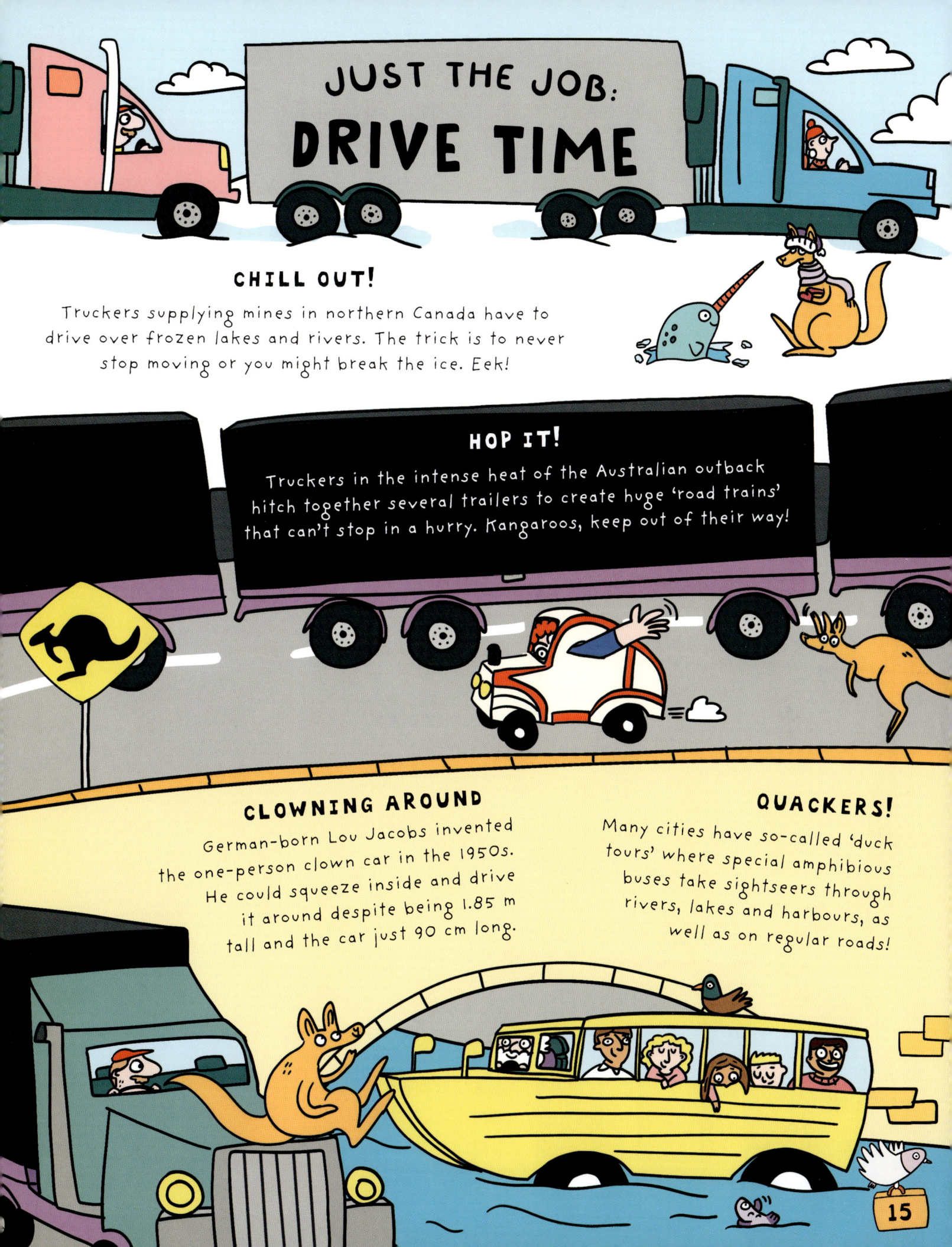

THE DAY JOB

BESSIE COLEMAN

NAME: BESSIE COLEMAN
NATIONALITY: AMERICAN
OCCUPATION: AVIATRIX

Hi! My name is Bessie Coleman. I was born in Atlanta, Texas, USA, in 1892, one of thirteen children. What's an **aviatrix**? Well, keep reading and you'll find out!

In my early 20s, I moved to Chicago and worked in a beauty parlour. World War I was underway and soldiers back from France told me they had seen something amazing...

Women pilots! I was so excited. If men could become aviators, then I wanted to be an **aviatrix** – a female flyer. But no one would teach me because I was Black and a woman.

PFFH!

But I showed them. I studied French at night school and in 1920 I took my savings and sailed to France to take flying lessons in Paris. Magnifique!

SPACEMAN

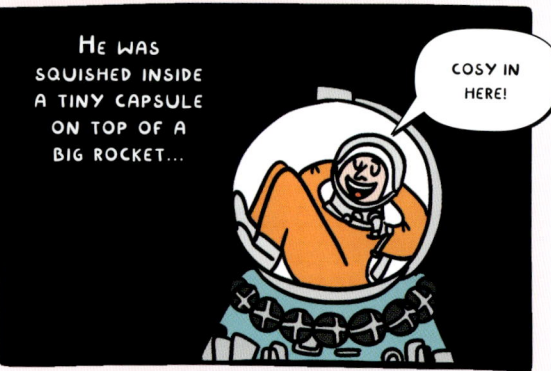

JUST THE JOB: GIMME SOME SPACE!

STAR TURNS
Over 40 countries have now sent people into space. In 1992, Mae Jemison became the first African-American female astronaut and took with her a picture of Bessie Coleman (see pages 16–17).

THIS JOB STINKS!
NASA actually employs people to sniff objects on Earth to check their smell won't annoy astronauts in space. Phooey!

SOFT JOBS
Soft toys play a part in space travel, floating about harmlessly when zero-gravity conditions have been reached. And they are fun!

ASLEEP ON THE JOB
Any future trip to Mars will take at least seven months. US space agency NASA pays people to sleep for weeks to see what effect prolonged rest has on their bodies.

TASTE OF SPACE
The European Space Agency (ESA) asked French chefs to create dishes using crops that might grow on Mars. The result? Pond slime pasta (yum!) and a Martian bread with green tomato jam.

19

WORLD OF WONDERS: BROUGHT TO BOOK

Books are brilliant. They can take you to another place without ever leaving your seat. Better still, mobile libraries can bring you fresh books for free! Check these out!

In Colombia, the **Biblioburro**, ('donkey library') brings books to remote villages. Two donkeys — Alfa and Beto — do the, er, donkey work.

In Mongolia, **camels** carry books to desert-dwelling nomads. No need to be lost for words!

In Laos, librarians ride **elephants** to bring books to schools — an unforgettable experience!

In Argentina, an artist turned a car into a **tank** that drives round offering free books. Take cover!

In southern Italy, a retired teacher travels round in a bright blue **book house** with a tiled roof and a little chimney. Smoking!

Books ahoy! Remote islands in Sweden get visited twice a year by the **bokbåten** ('book boat').

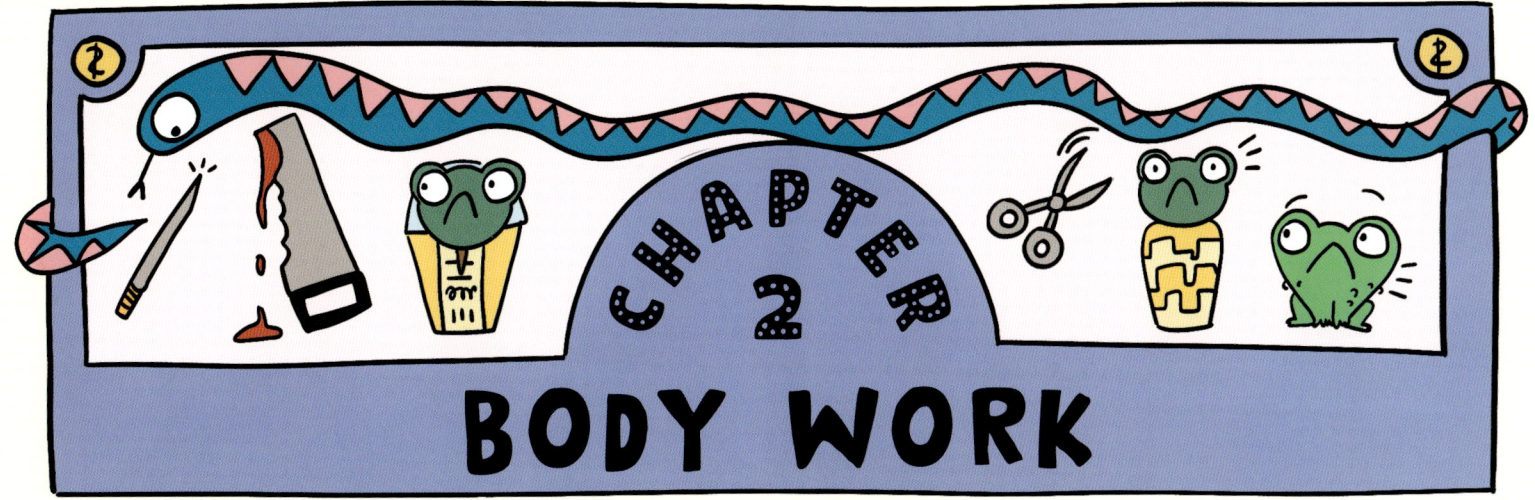

CHAPTER 2
BODY WORK

The human body is a brilliant bit of kit. There are tons of tasks it can take on, as well as providing jobs for people who claim they can fix it when it breaks down — not all of them honest or reliable! This chapter gets a bit grisly in places, but if you've got the guts for it, let's work that body — beginning with four fab facts!

OLDEST KNOWN SURGERY

A skeleton found in Borneo had successfully had a foot removed 31,000 years ago, when only stone tools existed! Ug!

REST IN PIECES

Three hundred years ago, thieves known as body-snatchers stole corpses from fresh graves to sell to medical students who then cut them up.

HANDY WORK

You don't have to show your face to get a top job in TV and films. Some people have lovely hands and get paid to show them in close-up shots.

BENDIEST BODY

Nicknamed 'The Rubberboy', US professional contortionist Daniel Browning Smith has super-flexible joints and can even turn his head behind him like an owl!

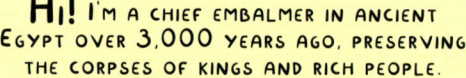

JUST THE JOB: WORK LIKE AN ANCIENT EGYPTIAN

SAD BUSINESS

Ancient Egyptian funerals might be attended by professional mourners — women paid to wail with grief. To do the job, they had to be childless. Being a real mummy was not allowed!

IT'S A STEAL

Tomb robber was a profitable job in ancient Egypt, stealing the treasures placed in pyramids alongside mummified royals. The objects in museums today are the things they missed!

MONKEY BUSINESS

Not all thieves got away with their crimes. Egyptian officials used trained baboons to catch suspects. It's the long tail of the law!

WORKING MUMMIES

Being dead didn't stop mouldy old mummies being useful. Millions of mummies were made, and in the past they were turned into brown paint and magic 'medicine'.

MOUSEWORK

Cats worked hard keeping homes and the harvest safe from hungry rats and mice. No wonder they were worshipped as gods and also made into mummies!

BARBER-SURGEON

JUST THE JOB: CURIOUS CURERS

POLE POSITION
As well as lopping limbs, barber-surgeons let blood out of people's bodies. The striped poles outside many modern barbers represent the bloody bandages involved.

SO LONG, SUCKERS!
Water-living worms called leeches were also used to suck blood from patients. Leech collectors stood bare-legged in lakes to attract them.

DOCTOR DOG
Dogs are more than just our best buds — they can be trained to sniff out diseases and bring people medicines. What cat would do that?

THE HOLE STORY
Prehistoric people drilled holes in skulls to let out 'evil spirits'. Surgeons use the same technique, called 'trepanation', today to help some head injuries heal!

FLY GUYS
Maggots are flies in the making. Disgusting as it sounds, they are used to clear dead flesh from wounds so they mend more quickly.

25

TOAD EATER

JUST THE JOB: THE FRAUD SQUAD

NAMED AND SHAMED
Because they climbed onto benches to work, fake doctors were called 'mountebanks', and toad eaters became 'toadies', a word used today for an over-keen assistant.

RATTLING GOOD TAIL
A 'snake oil merchant' was another trickster selling fake medicine. Former US cowboy Clark Stanley called himself the 'Rattlesnake King', but his 'miracle cure' actually contained no snake oil at all! Boo! Hiss!

THE CON IS ON (AND ON AND ON)
Several fraudsters have 'sold' famous buildings they didn't own. In the last century, Czech rogue Victor Lustig 'sold' the Eiffel Tower twice, while an Indian master of disguise known as Natwarlal 'sold' the Taj Mahal thrice!

THE CAT'S PYJAMAS?
US professional hoaxer Alan Abel made a career out of pranking the press. In the 1960s, he made world news with a pretend campaign to clothe naked animals. It had the slogan: 'A nude horse is a rude horse'!

27

THE DAY JOB

WAXWORK MAKER

NAME: MARIE TUSSAUD
NATIONALITY: FRENCH
OCCUPATION: WAXWORK MAKER

MARIE TUSSAUD

Bonjour! My name is Madame Marie Tussaud and, over 170 years after my death, I am still the most famous waxwork maker ever. No one can hold a candle to me!

I was born in Strasbourg, France, in 1761. Aged six, my mother became housekeeper to a Swiss doctor who also made wax figures. He taught me everything. I was a model pupil!

At 15, I completed my first full figure, of the big French thinker Voltaire. Other models followed, and one day I was asked to move to the royal Palace of Versailles to teach wax-modelling to King Louis XVI's sister, Elisabeth.

Sadly, ordinary French citizens were starving while the rich lived in luxury. I mean, look at this place!

In 1789, the French people revolted, took over the country, and eventually arrested the whole royal family — and me! Lots of nobles lost their heads on the guillotine.

I might well have lost mine too, only I was spared and asked to make wax masks of the dead heads in the executioner's basket. Including those of the king and queen!

France went wild for a while, so I moved to Britain and toured my waxworks around the country. Most popular was my figure of French Emperor Napoleon Bonaparte. For a little man, he was a big attraction!

I eventually settled into a museum in London, and in 1842 I made a model of myself which you can still see today! When it came to making waxworks, I broke the mould!

HUMANOID

JUST THE JOB: REAL LIVE WIRES

SEAL OF APPROVAL
Developed in Japan, PARO is a cuddly robotic baby seal that interacts with patients in nursing homes. PARO's battery charger looks like a baby's dummy!

SPACE-TALK
In 2013, Kirobo was the first robot to speak in space. Just 34 cm tall, he chatted to Koichi Wakata, the first Japanese commander of the International Space Station.

OH, BROTHER!
In 2010, robot expert Hiroshi Ishiguro made a twin robot of himself. Unlike a real baby brother, you could turn him off!

NOT TO BE SNEEZED AT
Launched in 2014, Pepper is a robot that can respond to human emotions. Thousands of friendly Peppers now work in banks and airports.

BRIGHT DAWN
DAWN is a Tokyo cafe where robot waiters are controlled remotely using the eye movements of people suffering from paralysis who cannot leave home to work.

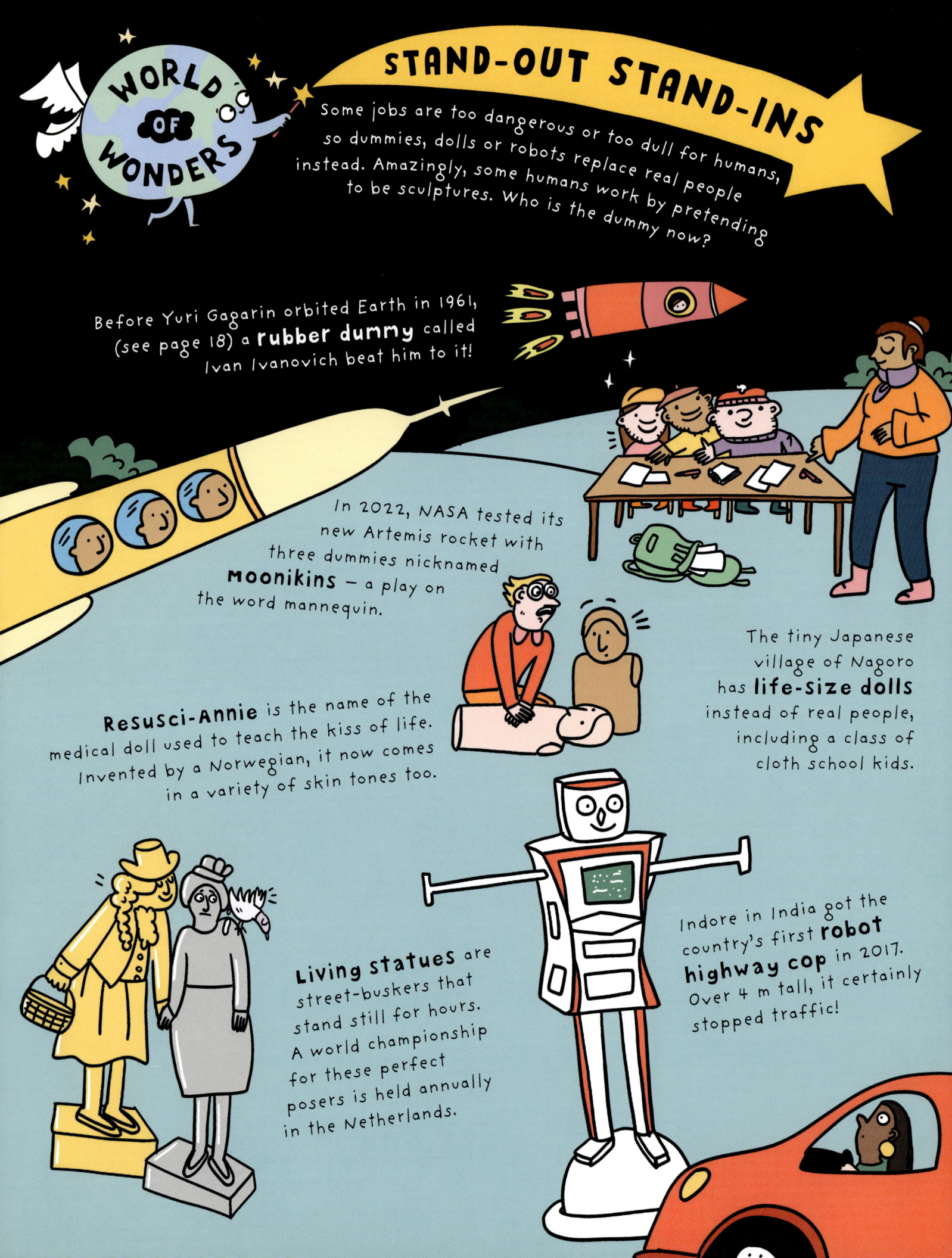

CHAPTER 3
NICE WORK

Royals have long been the envy of less lucky humans. Compared to most working people, they had it easy. Today, some people still dream of being king or queen, but others want to be pop stars, social media influencers or perhaps even authors and illustrators! This chapter is about jobs that just seem better than others — beginning with four very cushy numbers.

LONGEST SERVING ROYAL

Louis XIV had France's top job for 72 years and 110 days. He held court squatting on a potty built into a throne, which is what you can do when you're king.

JUST WATCH IT!

Streaming giant Netflix pays people to watch its shows and 'tag' them so others can find new things to view. You call that work?!

BEST JOB EVER?

In 2014, a Chinese wildlife sanctuary advertised for a 'panda nanny' to cuddle newborn pandas. Unsurprisingly, over 100,000 people applied!

NEXT BEST JOB EVER?

American John Harrison spent 30 years as an ice cream tester. He used a golden spoon and insured his taste buds for $1 million US dollars!

 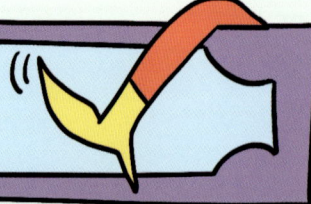

COURT JESTER

JUST THE JOB: JEST FOR LAUGHS

BLOWN AWAY

Roland the Farter was jester to medieval English king Henry II. His job was simple: every Christmas he entertained the court with 'one jump, one whistle and one fart'. In return, he was given a huge country house. (Now see page 86!)

SILVER LINING

Shen Jiangao, jester to 10th-century Chinese emperor Liezu, famously joked during a drought that rain would not fall because the emperor might tax it. Legend says the emperor cut taxes as a result, and it rained the very next day.

NO LAUGHING MATTER

Mathurine the Fool was a female jester at the French court in the 16th century. She dressed as a warrior from the Amazon region of South America, and once helped foil an attempt to kill the French king Henry IV.

BELL-Y LAUGHS

In 1999, the King of Tonga appointed an American businessman, Jesse Bogdonoff, to be the official jester to his island nation. His duties included wearing the traditional three-pointed coxcomb hat, complete with bells.

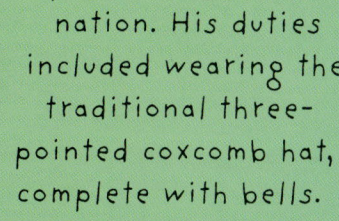

PLUTOCRAT

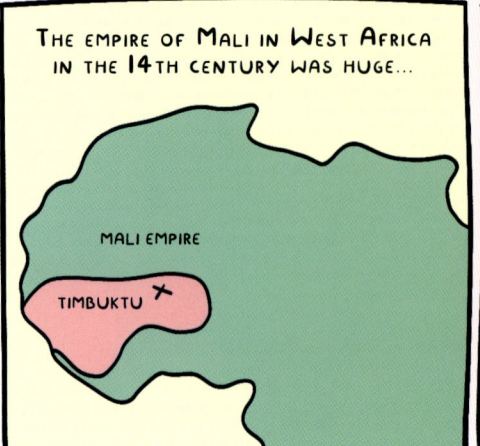

The empire of Mali in West Africa in the 14th century was huge...

MALI EMPIRE
TIMBUKTU

I'm its ruler, Mansa Musa, and I'm a plutocrat.

No, that doesn't mean I'm keen on dwarf planets or goofy-looking cartoon dogs*...

NOPE!
WRONG!

* NO COPYRIGHT INFRINGEMENT!

It means I am incredibly, stupendously, unimaginably wealthy...

MINE, ALL MINE - AND THIS IS ONLY A TINY BIT OF IT...

In fact, I'm the richest person ever to have lived. Far richer than this modern lot put together...

Rainforest-named online shop guy

Rocket man

Computer software supremo

Singing sensation!

In 1324, I decided to go on a religious pilgrimage to Mecca...

I SHALL DO THE HAJJ.
GOOD IEDA, YOUR MAJ!

I took a caravan of tens of thousands of soldiers, slaves, entertainers, sheep, goats and 100 camels, each laden with 136 kg of gold...

TRUST US TO GET STUCK BEHIND A CARAVAN...
THIS GOLD IS SOOO HEAVY.
IT'S GIVING ME THE HUMP!

Along the journey, I simply gave the precious metal away... kilos of gold...

IS THIS A SCAM?
NO, GOOD AS GOLD, MATE.

When I returned, I built universities and mosques – some of which still stand...

DJINGUEREBER MOSQUE, TIMBUKTU

But best of all, I put Mali and me on the map – literally!

GOLD STAR FOR ME, I THINK!

JUST THE JOB: POWER MAD?

ARE EWE KIDDING?
French queen Marie Antoinette had a cute model farm built in the grounds of the royal palace so she could play at shepherding lambs. She herself got the chop soon afterwards! (See page 29.)

CASTLES IN THE AIR
In the 19th century, King Ludwig II of Bavaria (now part of Germany) spent big bucks building fairy-tale castles. Some said he was mad, but today tourists love them!

STICKY SITUATION
Ancient Egyptian pharaoh Pepi II hated flies so much he had someone stand, coated in honey, in every room so they would bother them instead of him. Buzz off!

DIY, HRH?
Many claims have been made about the daily duties servants perform for the UK's King Charles III. These include ironing his shoelaces, squeezing his toothpaste, and correctly positioning his bathplug.

37

HERMIT

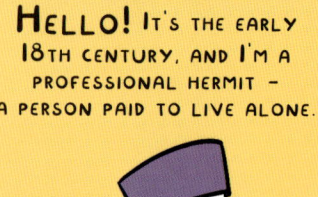  

JUST THE JOB: LIMITED COMPANY

GUIDING LIGHT

Sally Snowman (her real name!) is the USA's last lighthouse keeper. Her lighthouse on a tiny Massachusetts island dates back to the 1700s, and she dresses in clothes from the period!

STRICTLY FOR THE BIRDS

The 'guardian' of Gabo Island, off the coast of Australia, is its only human resident. However, there are 30,000 little penguins to keep them company. Squawk!

OFF THE RAILS!

Freight trains in India can be over 2 km in length! Both the engine driver at the front and the guard in the rear wagon are totally alone on long, slow journeys through the jungle.

FAR AND AWAY

Concordia scientific research station in Antarctica is one of the world's most remote workplaces. The crew of the International Space Station are actually closer to other human beings!

THE DAY JOB

GRUMPY CAT

INTERNET CELEBRITY

NAME: TARDAR SAUCE (AKA GRUMPY CAT)
NATIONALITY: CAT
OCCUPATION: INTERNET CELEBRITY

Hello. Pleased to meet you, even if I don't look like it. That's what made me famous: I'm a sourpuss puss, known to millions by my showbiz name, Grumpy Cat.

I was one of a litter of kittens born in Arizona, USA, in 2012. My 'owner' (she thinks!) was called Tabatha Bundesen, but it was her brother Bryan who you could say 'let the cat out of the bag'.

In September 2012 he posted this snap on an internet news site, and it went viral — I think that's the right word. Frankly, I've been uninterested in computers since I discovered their mice are inedible.

People began sharing images of me and adding words as if they were my thoughts.

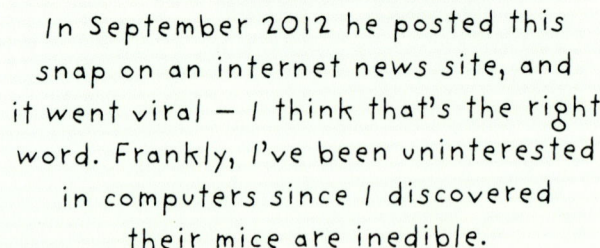
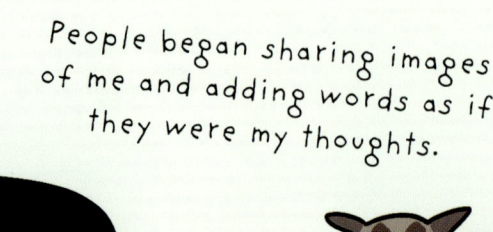

CHAPTER 4
RISKY BUSINESS

Some jobs are dream jobs, some are a nightmare — difficult to do and dangerous with it. Throughout history, really risky work has tended to be forced upon forced upon the poor or enslaved, or people in prison — and women. Working animals, too, have been in danger of death or injury. So, let's start this chapter as safely as possible with four fearful facts.

WORLD'S RISKIEST DISHES

Ancient Roman emperors made food tasters check their meals weren't poisoned. Despite this, Emperor Claudius died from poisoned mushrooms in 54 BCE.

NO LAUGHING MATTER

Hat-making might sound safe, but 200 years ago the toxic chemicals used made people ill, hence the Mad Hatter in *Alice in Wonderland*.

BREAKING NEWS

US stunt performer Evel Knievel was famous in the 1970s for attempting crazy motorcycle jumps. He holds the world record for most bones broken: 433 times!

BIOLOGY LESSON

Teaching is a safe profession, though there are occasional surprises. In 2022, a very cross cougar turned up in the toilets of a Brazilian school!

NORSE FARMER

JUST THE JOB: NORSE POWER

KEY WORKERS
Norse women ran the farms while their husbands were off raiding. They held the keys to all the doors and treasure chests, and were often buried with a bundle of keys to show their high status.

MAD FOR IT
Perhaps the scariest Viking warriors were the 'berserkers', who dressed in bear-furs and ate poisonous plants to put them into a rage before fighting. They really did go berserk!

CARVING OUT A LIVING
Viking craftspeople carved ivory from the tusks of walruses, like the famous Isle of Lewis chess pieces. An ancient ivory carver was called a schrimpschonger!

CLIFFHANGER
Vikings ate seabird eggs that were collected from their nests by lowering plucky egg collectors down the sides of steep cliffs on long ropes.

DON'T FORGET!
Poets held an important position in Viking society — but you needed a good memory for the job as none of their myths were written down.

PIRATE

JUST THE JOB: DEEP WATER

MISSING PERSONS
American cargo ship Mary Celeste was found drifting and deserted in the Atlantic Ocean in 1872. Her lifeboat was gone and her crew were never found. Some claim she was attacked by a giant squid!

MONKEY BUSINESS
Children had one of the most dangerous jobs on a pirate ship. Called 'powder monkeys', they ran around bringing fresh gunpowder and ammunition during sea battles. Scary!

IT TAKES GUTS
Deep-sea fishing is one of the world's most dangerous jobs today. Wet decks are slippery, especially when covered with smelly fish guts. The window squeegee was developed from a tool for scraping them into the sea.

PERILOUS PEARLS
Ama are Japanese women that free-dive into the freezing cold sea to harvest pearls from oysters down below. Their traditional white outfits are said to frighten off sharks!

HUNGRY HIPPOS?
Fishermen on the shores of Lake Naivasha in Kenya don't worry about sharks. Instead they look out for angry hippopotamuses, which attack thousands of Africans every year.

THE DAY JOB

ZAZEL

HUMAN CANNONBALL

NAME: ZAZEL
NATIONALITY: BRITISH
OCCUPATION: HUMAN CANNONBALL

Hello! Can you imagine getting fired every day? Well, that's what happened to me as the world's first human cannonball. I was shot out of a giant cannon, sometimes twice a day, for entertainment!

My stage name was 'Zazel', but my real name is Rossa Matilda Richter. I was born in London in 1860, and was tightrope-walking at the age of six. Life really was a circus!

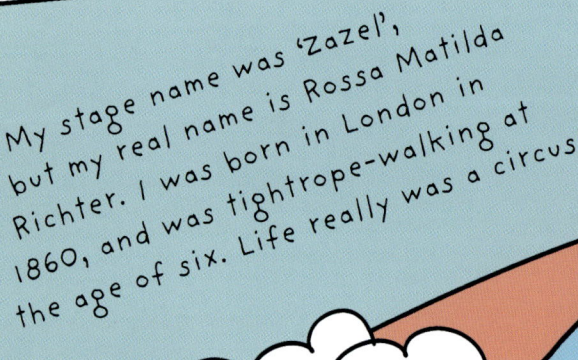

In 1877, aged 17, my career took a new direction — upwards! A showman calling himself 'The Great Farini' (real name Bill Hunt!) shot me 20 m across a stage to the delight of audiences. Business boomed!

The newspapers called me the 'Miss who was a Missile' and there were even songs written about me. I was a star! A shooting star!

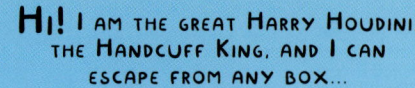

JUST THE JOB: HOW DARE YOU?

IN THE BALANCE

Niagara Falls, the giant waterfall between the USA and Canada, is a magnet for professional daredevils. In 1859, French acrobat Charles Blondin was the first person to tightrope walk across the gorge. He also went over on stilts and pushing a wheelbarrow!

BASKET WORK

Italian Maria Spelterini is the only woman to have tightrope walked the Falls. In 1876, she crossed blindfolded, and once with her feet in baskets!

BARREL OF FUN

In 1901, American Annie Edson Taylor rode the Falls in a large oak barrel and, amazingly, survived the 50-m drop. She was 63 — and a former schoolteacher!

CROSS COUNTRY

Stunts at the Falls were banned after several tragic accidents. However, in 2012 American Nik Wallenda was allowed to attempt the first wire-walk for 116 years. He took along his passport to show on the Canadian side.

BOUNCING BACK

Canadian Jean Lussier went over the Falls in a giant inflatable rubber ball in 1928. He then made a living selling pieces of it to tourists.

JUST THE JOB: PAWS FOR THOUGHT

BIRD BRAINS
The PDSA, a British veterinary charity, awards its Dickin Medal to brave working animals. Its first three winners in 1943 were all homing pigeons who helped rescuers find crashed aircraft and save their crews during World War II.

HOOFING IT
The novel War Horse by Michael Morpurgo was made into a hit movie. In 2014, a real war horse called Warrior was given the Dickin Medal on behalf of all the brave animals of World War I, 100 years earlier.

TOP CAT
Simon is the only cat with a Dickin Medal. In 1949, despite being injured, he kept food supplies on board the British warship HMS Amethyst safe from rats after it was hit by a missile. In return, he was made 'Able Seaman Simon'.

DAREDEVIL DOG
A dog called Satan was a French hero of World War I. Wearing a gas mask, and despite being shot in the leg, he got a vital message through to trapped troops at the Battle of Verdun.

REARGUARD ACTION
Sergeant Stubby of the US Infantry was the most decorated dog of World War I. He helped warn of poison gas attacks, and once held an enemy soldier by the seat of his trousers!

53

CHAPTER 5
WORKING WONDERS

In the far past, humans were super superstitious. They trusted priests, wise women, and other mystics to protect them from bad stuff, as well as predict the future. Today, we think we know better, but jobs that involve mysterious powers won't be going out of business anytime soon. Here are four facts to start us off.

MOST FAMOUS FORECASTER

French astrologer Nostradamus wrote weird poems in the 1550s that some claim predicted future events such as the Great Fire of London and World War II.

DOWSE THAT!

In the 1950s, British dowser Evelyn Penrose was asked to locate hidden oil wells by swinging a pendulum over maps of land thousands of miles away!

HOW TOUCHING!

In medieval France and England, it was the job of a king or queen to touch people with diseases, as royals were said to have magical healing powers!

RUN OF LUCK

In 1920s America, Lady Wonder was a famous mind-reading horse who used her nose to type out prophecies. She even forecast winning racehorses!

JUST THE JOB: FORTUNE-SELLERS

CHICKEN FEED
Ancient Roman armies consulted a fortune-teller before going into battle. They threw corn to sacred chickens and if the birds didn't eat, then they didn't fight. Chicken?

SET IN STONE
Vikings scattered stones known as runes bearing letters from the Norse alphabet to read the future. Ask the runes, "Should we go raiding?" and the answer seems to have often been "Yes". (See page 44.)

NUT JOB
Obi is an ancient West African prediction method. Fortune-tellers throw kola nuts — seeds of the kola tree — to see how they land. The nuts have also given their name to fizzy cola.

COOKIES ENABLED
Fortune cookies date back to the 19th century. Three billion get baked each year, so cookie companies always need new writers for the slips placed inside them.

HAVING A BALL
Magic 8 Ball is an American fortune-telling toy. Inside the ball is a 20-sided dice that floats up to a little window where its answer can be read. Spooky!

THE DAY JOB

JAMES RANDI

NAME: JAMES RANDI
NATIONALITY: CANADIAN/AMERICAN
OCCUPATION: CHARLATAN

Hi! I'm James Randi, and I'm a **charlatan** — a word for a cheat or trickster. I can't work any wonders, so what am I doing here? Good question! Always ask questions!

I was born Randall James Hamilton Zwenge in Canada in 1928. I shortened it to James Randi but I was better known as The Amazing Randi! Let me explain...

When I was a teenager, I had a bad accident and was bed-bound for a year, so I read lots of books about magic. One of my heroes was the Great Houdini (see page 50). Later, I copied some of his tricks!

Anyway, I recovered and at 17 started work as a magician, reading people's minds on stage.

Yes, it was just a trick, but my knowledge meant I could challenge others who pretended they did it for 'real'.

PROGNOSTICATOR

CHAPTER 6
WORK HARD, PLAY HARD

The human race: the name says it all, really. People are always trying to outdo each other. In the past, the person who could throw a spear the farthest would have been the most valuable hunter. Nowadays it's the superstars of track and field who get the gold medals. In this chapter, we look at sports, some rather risky, beginning with four world-class facts.

WORLD'S MOST POPULAR SPORT

Association football — known as football, for short — has over 4 billion fans across the planet. In fact, the planet is even football-shaped!

OLDEST PRO-ATHLETE

Polish veteran Stanislav Kowalski became the world's oldest professional competitor in 2014 for the 100 metres, discus and shot put. He was 104 years old, making all his results world records!

ODDEST OLYMPIC EVENTS

Since the modern Games began in 1896, it has included tug of war, ballooning, rope-climbing, and ski-ballet. Video-gamers hope to compete in the future!

MOST SUCCESSFUL PARALYMPIAN

Blind American swimmer Trischa Zorn-Hudson won 55 medals across seven Paralympic Games from 1980 onwards, 41 of them gold. Her record will probably never be beaten!

JUST THE JOB: GREEK EARNERS

STRIP NAKED
Women weren't allowed to compete – or even watch the Olympic Games. However, one woman called Pherenike dressed as a man to watch her son compete. She was found out when she got so excited her disguise fell off!

BULLY FOR HIM
Milo of Croton won the Olympic wrestling title six times in total from 540 BCE onwards. Legend has it he once carried a bull on his shoulders around the stadium.

BLOW YOUR OWN!
The ancient Olympics included arts events. Herodorus of Megara won the trumpet event 10 times, thanks to the sheer loudness of his playing. PAAAARP!

FOOT SOLDIER
Leonidas of Rhodes won 12 foot races from 164 BCE onwards, making him the greatest ancient Olympian. One of his events, the hoplitodromos, involved running in bronze armour with a heavy shield!

FALL FROM GRACE
Theagenes of Thasos was a hugely successful boxer, winning over 1,000 bouts. A statue of Theagenes fell on a jealous rival boxer, killing them. The statue was then tried for murder, found guilty, and thrown into the sea!

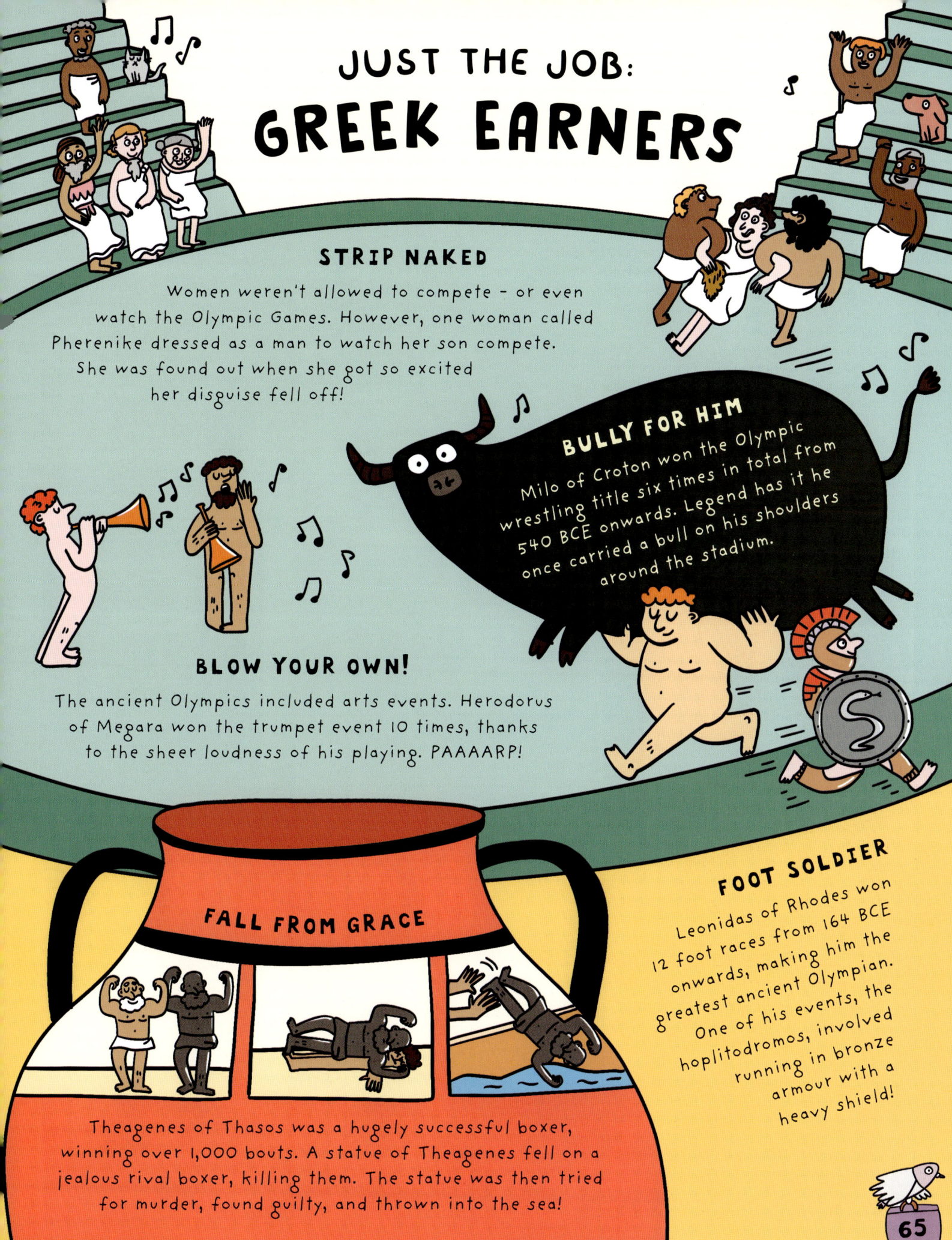

JUST THE JOB: INJURY TIME

CHEESE ROLL
Cheese-rolling is a wild and dangerous sport which happens every year at Cooper's Hill in Gloucestershire, UK. People chase a wheel of cheese down a steep hill. The first to the bottom wins the cheese, even though most end up with bumps and bruises!

GLOVE STORY
As its name suggests, chessboxing is a mix of chess and boxing, originally invented for a comic book story. Players switch between a boxing bout in the ring and an ongoing chess match on a table placed alongside.

SNOW JOKE!
Snowboarding is one of the most dangerous sports in the modern Olympics. To add extra thrills, you can slide down the slopes of Mauna Kea, a super-high snow-capped volcano in Hawaii!

IRON MAN
Extreme ironing was invented by a bored British mountaineer, Phil Shaw, in 1997. He had shirts to iron but preferred to spend his time rock climbing, so he combined the two!

TAG TEAM
Kabaddi is hugely popular in Asia. Two teams face off on a hard court while individual players race forward to tag their opponents before being tackled to the ground in a punishing pile-on.

THE DAY JOB

LILY PARR

FOOTBALLER

NAME: LILY PARR
NATIONALITY: BRITISH
OCCUPATION: FOOTBALLER

Hello! Want to know which football player scored almost 1,000 goals in their 30-year career? Well, it's me — Lily Parr. Back of the net!

I was born in a small town, called St Helens, in the north of England in 1905, but there was nothing small about me! I grew 1.8 m tall and being big, I could soon match my older brothers at football and rugby!

Aged 14, I started playing football for a local women's team, but was poached to play for a local factory's female team called the Dick, Kerr Ladies. Begun in 1917, they soon became world-famous.

Back then, men were away fighting in World War I, so the factory formed the female football team to entertain people. Under captain Alice Kell, their matches raised huge sums for charity. And players got paid!

WORLD OF WONDERS

COSTUME DRAMA

Lots of jobs involve special workwear, such as firefighters, nurses and the police. The people who dress as mascots at sporting events take this to the extreme, adding to the fun and excitement. Fancy fitting into any of these outfits?

The mascot for the 2023 Women's Football World Cup in Australia and New Zealand was a **penguin called Tazuni**. Lily Parr would be pleased!

Bouncer, a **big green ball** with purple shades, was chosen as the mascot for the Caribbean Cricket Premier League.

Olly, a furry version of a rare **olive Ridley turtle**, is the mascot for all sports events in Odisha, India, including the 2023 Hockey World Cup.

Scottish football side Partick Thistle has a scary **sun-shaped mascot** called Kingsley. Luckily, fans have taken a shine to him!

The mascot of the Spanish football team CD Leganes is a 2-m tall pickle known as the **Cucumber Knight**. Cool!

Nazo No Sakana ('Mysterious Fish') is the mascot for Japanese baseball team the Chiba Lotte Marines. It often evolves and changes shape!

CHAPTER 7
ARTS WORK

Humans have been singing, dancing, painting and creating other forms of art for thousands of years — even our relatives, the Neanderthals, decorated caves with depictions of animals. Today, the arts is a huge industry from poetry and drama to music, TV, films and video games. In this chapter, human creativity takes centre stage, with four fab facts as our opening acts.

DOTS TO SPACE SPOTS!

In the past, Neanderthals painted coloured dots on cave walls. In 2003, tiny dots painted by British artist Damien Hirst landed on Mars on board the *Beagle 2* spacecraft. Time flies!

MOST WATCHED MUSIC VIDEO

'Baby Shark dance', launched in 2016 by the South Korean Pinkfong Company, now has over 15 billion views on a planet with a population of 8 billion people! Doo-doo, doo-doo!

BEST-SELLING CHILDREN'S BOOK

Not *Harry Potter*, but *The Little Prince* by French aristocrat Antoine de Saint-Exupéry. Since 1943, this tale of a crashed pilot and a golden-haired boy who lives on an asteroid has sold over 200 million copies.

PRICIEST PIXEL

Everydays: The First 5000 Days is a collage of 5,000 digital images by American artist Mike 'Beeple' Winkelmann. You can't hang it on your wall, but it sold in 2021 for $69 million!

ACTOR

JUST THE JOB: ACT ON IT!

TRADING PLACES

In Britain, Christmas pantomimes are funny family shows where the top female role of 'Dame' is played by a man in a crazy costume, while a woman plays the lead part of 'Principal Boy'. Pairs of actors also pretend to be comedy cows and horses!

DEAD CLEVER

Many TV shows and films need someone to play a corpse. Lying still without breathing or blinking is a special skill — one that US actor Chuck Lamb specialised in since 2005 as the 'Dead Body Guy'!

LADDIE FETCH HELP!

Clever animation and puppets are now often used in films instead of actual living animal actors as training can be very expensive. Lassie, perhaps the most famous female film dog ever, was originally played by a male dog called Pal!

THE NEXT STAGE?

A science museum in Krakow, Poland, puts on short plays performed by a cast of robots known as RoboThespians, after Thespis, a famous ancient Greek actor. Will robots one day put actors out of work?

MODERN ARTIST

Hi! I'm a type of men's toilet called a urinal.

NOT PRETTY, EH?

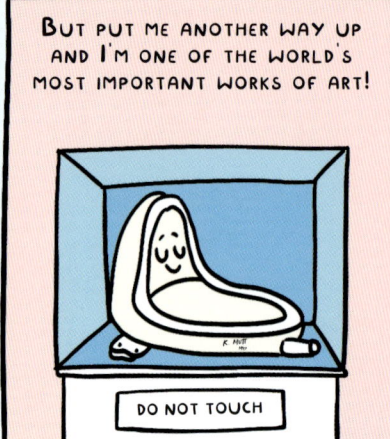

But put me another way up and I'm one of the world's most important works of art!

DO NOT TOUCH

And this French guy is one of the world's most important artists ever — Marcel Duchamp.

SOMETIMES KNOWN AS MY FEMALE OTHER ME, 'ROSE SÉLAVY'.

In 1917, Marcel was living in New York, USA, when he bought me brand new from a plumbing shop and added a simple signature and the year.

R. MUTT 1917

Voila! I was transformed into a work of modern art that he called 'Fountain'.

FUNNY NAME FOR A URINAL, HUH?

This was a new way of working for artists, one based on ideas alone.

I CALLED THIS CONCEPT AN, ER, 'CONCEPT'.

Marcel named his creations 'readymades' – found or bought objects, often left unchanged but with a new way of thinking about them...

A COAT-RACK ON THE FLOOR

'TRAP'

A BOTTLE DRIER

'HEDGEHOG'

A SNOW SHOVEL

'IN ADVANCE OF A BROKEN ARM'

A BIKE WHEEL ON A BAR STOOL

'BICYCLE WHEEL'

He even 'improved' a print of one of the world's most famous paintings...

WE ARE NOT AMUSED — OR ARE WE?

Most of his original readymades were lost, but nowadays, later copies he made go for a fortune.

SOLD FOR $1.76 MILLION!

BANG!

...which is why I'm now under a protective glass case!

AT LEAST IT MEANS NO ONE CAN WEE ON ME!

JUST THE JOB: RUBBISH ARTISTS

TOP DRAWER

Born in Yokohama, Japan, sculptor Sayaka Ganz combines thrown-away household utensils such as spoons and spatulas to create amazing models of animals in action.

METAL WORKER

Ghanaian-born artist El Anatsui is famous for his 'bottle-top installations' — large sheet-like sculptures made from thousands of small pieces of reclaimed metal sewn together with wire.

ON A ROLL

Based in Berlin, Yuken Teruya works with waste paper and discarded toilet roll tubes to craft intricate sculptures that celebrate trees: the original sources of paper and card.

PET PROJECT

UK up-cycler Robert Bradford turns broken toys into playful pieces of art. Some sculptures contain over 3,000 components, and he can even portray people's pets!

JUST THE JOB: ROLE CRAWL

KEY GRIP
No, they don't hold the director's house keys. Grip crews organise all the equipment on a movie set, and the key grip organises all the grip crews. Get a grip!

BEST BOY
Or best girl — is second in rank to the gaffer ('best boy/girl electric') and to the key grip ('best boy/girl grip'). Despite the name, they will both be grown-ups!

GAFFER
Not the person in charge of mistakes, but the head electrician on a film production. You could say, they're a bright spark!

FOOD STYLIST
Makes fake food that stays looking good while scenes are shot over and over again. Mashed potato makes a good stand-in for ice cream!

FOLEY ARTIST
Adds sound effects to scenes, often faking them in clever ways, such as snapping a stick of celery for the sound of a broken bone! Ouch!

SEAT FILLER
At televised movie awards ceremonies, a smartly dressed person who sits in for a celebrity who needs the loo so the row still looks full. What a star!

FILL MY SEAT WHILE I EMPTY MY BLADDER!

SHH!

WRANGLER
Looks after on-screen children or animals and keeps them happy between takes. Baby wranglers can make babies cry on cue, often by crying themselves!

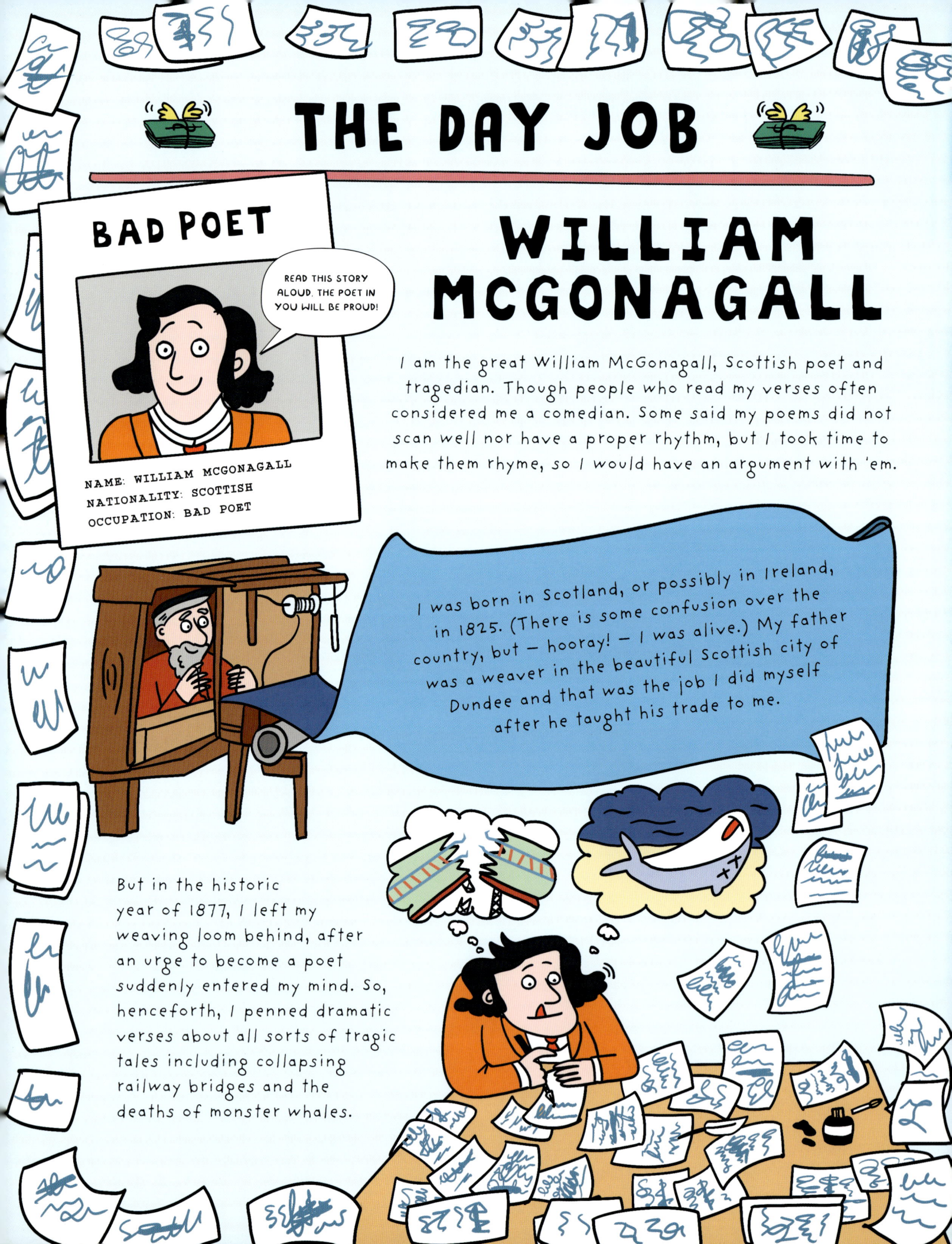

WORLD OF WONDERS

HANDIWORK

Puppetry is a form of theatre that was common in many ancient cultures across the world, and is still performed today. Here are some examples from countries with a hand in keeping it alive!

Wayang is a form of puppet theatre from the Indonesian island of Java. Rodded flat **leather puppets** cast shadows onto a white linen screen.

Yaya Coulibaly is a famous performer from Mali, West Africa — keeping alive an ancient tribal tradition. He has hundreds of puppets!

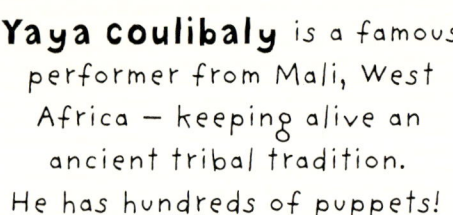

Punch and Judy is an old-fashioned British entertainment dating back to the 17th century. Puppeteers call themselves 'professors'.

Bunraku is a traditional Japanese show, with puppets operated by three people, often cloaked and hidden from view!

In Vietnam, audiences can enjoy **traditional tales** featuring puppets that perform scenes in water, including fishing, rice planting and duck herding.

CHAPTER 8
DIRTY WORK

"It's a dirty job, but someone's got to do it" is a popular saying — just bad luck if that person is YOU. Jobs involving poo, wee and other distasteful wastes are frequently frowned upon, though they can be vital and even well paid. This chapter holds its nose and peers from a distance at some of history's most horrible occupations, beginning with four foul facts.

THAR SHE BLOWS!

Canadian marine biologist Justine Hudson collects snot sprayed from the blowholes of Beluga whales. She scoops it from the sea to examine later in her laboratory.

WORLD'S BIGGEST BLOCKAGE?

In 2017, a 250-m long mass of old cooking fat and disposable nappies was cut free from London's sewers. The 'fatberg' took nine weeks to remove, and then went on display in a museum!

SORRY TO BRING THIS UP...

The ancient Romans had puke-collectors at banquets to collect vomit from guests who had eaten too much. Today, theme parks employ staff to clear the vomit from below rollercoaster rides.
Don't look up! (And wear a hat...)

GET A WIGGLE ON!

Maggot farming is a smelly business but might help save the planet. In South Africa, food and farm waste is turned into millions of maggots (fly larvae) that can be fed to chickens instead of ground-up fish taken from the sea.

81

 # FULLER

JUST THE JOB: PEE FOR PROFIT

TO BOLDLY GO

Urine is very valuable in space. If you fancy being an astronaut on the orbiting International Space Station, bear in mind the job involves drinking clean water recycled from the crew's wee by a clever machine. Cheers!

THE SOILS OF WAR

In 17th-century Europe, chemicals in wee were vital in making gunpowder. So-called 'saltpetre men' had the power to harvest wee-soaked soil from under the floors of farms and churches, as people often wet themselves during super-long sermons.

DYEING FOR A WEE?

Woad is a plant once used to produce a bright blue dye. Making it involved rotting leaves in urine, producing a smell so bad English queen Elizabeth I banned woad-dyers from working near her palaces!

URINE LUCK?

From Roman times and earlier, urimancers were fortune-tellers that predicted your future from bubbles in a bowl of wee. Big bubbles meant money coming in, small bubbles spelled troubles!

JUST THE JOB: WHAT A WASTE!

ROYAL FLUSH

Groom of the stool was once one of the most privileged positions in the English royal court, especially in Tudor times. It involved helping the king go to the toilet in a bowl hidden inside a fabric-covered stool, which is why today poos are also called stools.

OFF THE SCALE

In medicine, poos are clues to a person's health. Doctors worldwide use the Bristol Stool Scale chart to describe them, from Type 1 (tiny dry lumps) to Type 7 (runny liquid). Types 3 and 4 — soft sausages — are the ones to aim for!

PURE LUCK

In Victorian London, pure-finders walked the streets, picked up dog poo with their bare hands and popped it into lidded buckets. It was sold to be used in softening leather used for book covers. (Don't worry! This book uses card!)

JUMBO JOBS

In Thailand, elephant dung is collected by hand to make environmentally friendly paper that doesn't involve cutting down trees. The poo is packed with plant fibres that are turned into colourful craft paper.

I toured local music halls as 'Le Pétomane', which means 'The Farting Maniac'. Dressed smartly (I think one should look smart to fart), I let rip with my many impressive impressions.

Audiences loved it, cheering and laughing until tears rolled down their cheeks (the ones on their faces, I mean!).

GUFF! SNUFF!

At this point, I should explain that though I was farting furiously and ferociously, my act did not stink. In fact, I was able to simply move clean air in and out of my posterior at will. Indeed, I could expel it with enough force to blow out a candle — a highlight of my performance!

Anyway, in 1892 I became a star at the Moulin Rouge, the world-famous musical theatre in Paris. People flocked to see me, and I bent over backwards to entertain them. By now my act included farmyard animal noises as well as playing a small flute and an ocarina by fart power alone!

My success took me all over the world, and made me very rich. I bought a huge house, married and raised ten children. However, I stopped performing in 1914 at the outbreak of World War I and went back to baking. Fancy an 'air biscuit', anyone?

PAAAARP!

WORLD OF WONDERS

YOU HAD ONE JOB...

The world of work is not always wonderful. People are human (most of them), and they can — and will — make mistakes. Here are some of recent history's most famous fails.

ART FAILURE

French artist Henri Matisse created collages from cut paper towards the end of his career. One work, Le Bateau, was shown upside down by New York's Museum of Modern Art for 47 days in 1961 before a visitor spotted the mistake!

THE FARCE IS WITH YOU

Imagine acting in one of the most famous movies ever — and clumsily bumping your head on a door frame. That's what actor Laurie Goode did playing a Stormtrooper in 1977's sci-fi epic, Star Wars — Episode IV: A New Hope. He claimed tummy trouble made him do it!

NOT SO FAB FOUR

The Beatles, a band from the UK, are the most successful pop group ever, having sold over 290 million records. However, in January 1962, a boss at the Decca recording company turned down the chance to sign them up, saying: 'The Beatles have no future in show business.' Oops!

ASLEEP ON THE JOB

In 2013, a German bank clerk tried to transfer 64.20 euros to a customer's account, but fell asleep with their finger on a single key of their computer, the number '2'. As a result, they instead transferred 222,222,222.22 euros! The dozy mistake went unspotted for hours!

CAT-ASTROPHE!

In 2021, Texas lawyer Rod Ponton was on an important video call to an American courthouse, unaware that a filter on his computer had swapped his face for a fluffy white kitten with goo-goo eyes. A recording of his 'Lawyer Cat' chat went viral!

HOLY MOLY!

In 2020, Italian priest Paolo Longo also fell foul of video filters. Live-streaming a service for stuck-at-home worshippers, he was turned into a wizard with a pointy hat, a black-and-white cat, and also grew a bright pink moustache. Heavens!

NOT SO WIZARD

Can you imagine rejecting the best-selling series of books ever? Twelve publishers turned down *Harry Potter* before one — Bloomsbury — finally took it on. Even then, author J K Rowling was told, 'You'll never make any money out of children's books, Jo.' Expelliarmus!

SLICE OF LIFE

'The icing on the cake' can mean something extra-special. However, photos of crazily iced cakes are an internet celebration of epic failures, often involving simple misunderstandings. For example: Bakery: 'Want anything written on top?' Customer: 'Nothing, thank you'. End result: the words 'Nothing, thank you' piped across it!

EARLY STARTERS

Do you consider yourself lucky to go to school? The answer may depend on how tasty you find your school dinners, but for much of human history, most children went to work from an early age. Often these jobs were dirty, dangerous and sometimes deadly. As this last chapter shows, there have been lots of horrible jobs for juniors in the past, as well as some wonderful ways to make a living today. Which of these positions would you pick?

CROSSING SWEEPER
Horses filled the streets of big cities before motor cars, and those same horses then filled the streets with their poo. Gangs of poor children armed with brooms cleared poo from the paths of smartly dressed people in return for pennies.

WHIPPING BOY
Hard to believe, but it is said that English royal princes once had a boy who sat by them in lessons and took a beating from the teacher on their behalf if they made a mistake. To whip the future king would be considered treason.

CLIMBING BOY
In the 19th century, chimney sweeps across Europe employed 'climbing boys' to sweep soot from inside the narrowest parts of chimneys. Little better than slaves, many died from their awful working conditions.

MUDLARK
It might sound fun, but this was an awful occupation. In Victorian London, poor children scavenged in the mud of the river Thames in the hope of finding things they might sell, even though the river was basically a big open sewer.

MONARCH

Tutankhamen became an Egyptian pharaoh at age nine. In 1632, Christina was made queen of Sweden, aged six. In 1384, a 10-year-old girl called Jadwiga was crowned KING of Poland. Go figure!

EMPEROR

Two-year-old Puyi became the last emperor of Imperial China in 1908. As supreme ruler, he was both super spoilt and incredibly cruel: beating servants and having other people blow on his soup to cool it for him.

POP IDOL

South Korean K-pop is the world's fastest-growing music scene, with bands such as BTS, Twice and Blackpink now known all over the globe. K-pop stars are discovered as teenagers and taught the moves that make them famous.

FILM STAR

The Harry Potter films made stars of many young actors, including Emma 'Hermione' Watson. She remains one of the world's highest-earning actresses. Better still, she got turned into action figures!

SOCIAL MEDIA STAR

Teenage vloggers (video-bloggers) on video-sharing platforms such as Instagram and YouTube can have a huge influence on their audiences. In 2016, 13-year-old American JoJo Siwa had girls around the world copying her hair bows!

To return to the opening question, school is a great start in life. Sadly, many children around the world are still denied the chance, and have to work to help their families, some doing jobs as horrid as the worst ones shown here. Try and remember that next time your teacher sets you homework!

91

CAREER PATH

As you'll have read, the world of work has offered a wide range of jobs throughout history. Follow the questions below to see what occupation might be best for you!

START HERE:

Are you a robot?
- YES → **HUMANOID** Page 30
- NO → Would you prefer to work from home?
  - YES → Do you occasionally cough up furballs?
    - YES → **GRUMPY CAT** Page 40
    - NO → **HERMIT** Page 38
  - NO → Are you sporty?
    - YES → Okay with working naked?
      - YES → REALLY?
        - YES → **GREEK WRESTLER** Page 64
        - NO → Okay with the serious risk of injury?
          - YES → REALLY?
            - YES → **FOOTBALLER** Page 68
            - NO → Very sensible
          - NO → Get on well with horses?
            - YES → **CHARIOT RACER** Page 12
            - NO → **AZTEC BALL GAME PLAYER** Page 66
      - NO!
    - NO → (continues)
  - DON'T MIND → Would you be happy cutting up people?
    - YES → Dead people?
      - YES → **MUMMY MAKER** Page 22
      - NO → **BARBER-SURGEON** Page 24
    - NO → **SPACEMAN** Page 18

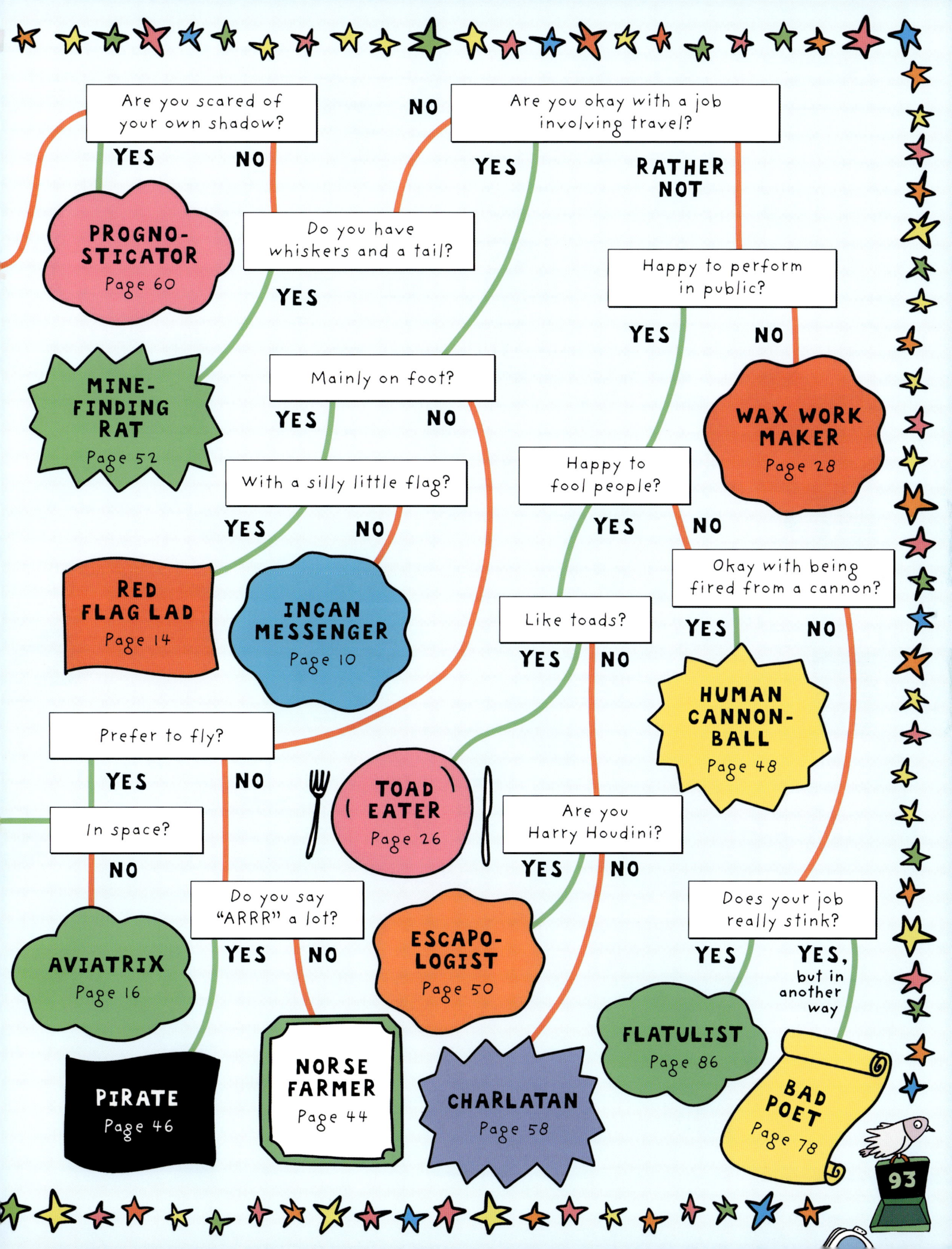

WORK'S LIKE A DREAM!

Is there a dream job that you'd love to have?
(Copy this page and fill in the spaces, ready to apply the moment it becomes available!)

CV

DRAW YOURSELF HERE

NAME AND AGE

....

DRAW YOUR DREAM JOB HERE:

DREAM JOB TITLE

....
....

WHY DO YOU WANT THIS JOB?

....
....
....
....
....

WHAT SKILLS CAN YOU BRING?

* ....
* ....
* ....
* ....
* ....
* ....
* ....

HOW MUCH WOULD YOU LIKE TO BE PAID?

....

THE JOB IS YOURS!

NOW, WHAT WILL YOU BUY WITH YOUR WAGES?